GEORGIA BULLDOGS

BY
RAMEY TEMPLE

INSIDE
COLLEGE
FOOTBALL

MEDIA ENHANCED BOOKS
AV² BY WEIGL™
ADDED VALUE • AUDIO VISUAL
www.av2books.com

AV^2 provides enriched content that supplements and complements this book. Weigl's AV^2 books strive to create inspired learning and engage young minds in a total learning experience.

Go to **www.av2books.com,** **and enter this book's unique code.**

BOOK CODE

AVK89288

AV^2 by Weigl brings you media enhanced books that support active learning.

Your AV^2 Media Enhanced books come alive with...

Audio
Listen to sections of the book read aloud.

Key Words
Study vocabulary, and complete a matching word activity.

Video
Watch informative video clips.

Quizzes
Test your knowledge.

Embedded Weblinks
Gain additional information for research.

Slideshow
View images and captions, and prepare a presentation.

Try This!
Complete activities and hands-on experiments.

... and much, much more!

Published by AV^2 by Weigl
350 5th Avenue, 59th Floor
New York, NY 10118
Website: www.av2books.com

Library of Congress Control Number: 2018968199

ISBN 978-1-7911-0065-0 (hardcover)
ISBN 978-1-7911-0066-7 (multi-user eBook)
ISBN 978-1-7911-0067-4 (single-user eBook)

Printed in Guangzhou, China
1 2 3 4 5 6 7 8 9 0 23 22 21 20 19

042019
102318

Project Coordinator: Jared Siemens Designer: Terry Paulhus

The publisher acknowledges Alamy, Getty Images, and Wikimedia Commons as its primary image suppliers for this title.

INSIDE COLLEGE FOOTBALL

Georgia Bulldogs

CONTENTS

Introduction

The University of Georgia (UGA) Bulldogs have been playing football for more than 100 years. Part of the Southeastern Conference (SEC), the Bulldogs have a very strong fan base with a history of successful head coaches. Spirited **rivalries** and long-standing traditions help make the Bulldogs a very celebrated football team.

The Bulldogs' story would not be complete without Vince Dooley, the head coach for an impressive 25 years. Under his leadership, and with the help of superstar running back Herschel Walker, the team went on to win many championships. When Dooley's reign was complete, he continued to help the football program. He was part of the team that hired Coach Mark Richt before the 2001 season. Coach Richt helped the Bulldogs continue to thrive.

Wide receiver Mecole Hardman scored both of Georgia's touchdowns in the 2018 College Football Playoff National Championship game against the University of Alabama.

With the arrival of Coach Kirby Smart in 2015, there have been high hopes for the beloved Bulldogs. After winning the Rose Bowl in 2018, the team has great momentum. Bulldogs fans everywhere are hoping to earn another national title.

Junior wide receiver Riley Ridley finished the 2017 season with 14 catches for 218 yards and two touchdowns for the Bulldogs.

GEORGIA

Stadium Sanford Stadium

Division Southeastern Conference (SEC) Eastern

Head Coach Kirby Smart

Location Athens, Georgia

National Championships 2

Nicknames Dawgs, UGA, Georgia, the Bulldogs

4
Hall of Fame Coaches

13
Conference Championships

2
Mascots

55
Bowl Games Played

History

In 1980, the Bulldogs were **undefeated** with a record of 12–0.

Georgia legend Herschel Walker is the only player in NCAA history to finish in the top three in Heisman voting for all three years of his college career. Walker won the Heisman Trophy in 1982.

Under the direction of head coach Dr. Charles Herty, the Georgia Bulldogs played their first game in 1892. Those early years laid the groundwork for some of Georgia's biggest rivalries. Auburn versus Georgia has been called "the South's oldest college football rivalry." The two teams first played in the late 1800s. The following year was the first game between Georgia and Georgia Tech, a rivalry known as "Clean, Old-Fashioned Hate."

In the late 1930s, Wally Butts was hired as head coach of Georgia. In 1942, the Bulldogs won the National Championship, and halfback Frank Sinkwich became Georgia's very first **Heisman Memorial Trophy** winner. In the 1960s, Coach Dooley led the team to six SEC championships. They won another National Championship in 1980. Several years later, Herschel Walker won the team's second Heisman.

Under the leadership of Coach Richt, the Bulldogs went on to win the SEC championship in both 2002 and 2005. Coach Smart led the Bulldogs to the SEC Championship Game and the National Championship in 2017, and the Rose Bowl in 2018. Today, the Bulldogs are ready to continue their domination and march toward another National Championship in college football.

Dr. Herty's first Georgia football team played two games in their first season, with a record of 1–1. The Bulldogs are one of the oldest college teams in the South.

The Stadium

Before the 1981 expansion of Sanford Stadium, hundreds of people watched games for free from railroad tracks that overlook the stadium's east end zone.

In the 1920s, after realizing that their home field was too small for the large crowds, the university decided to build the Bulldogs a new football stadium. Led by the university's president, Dr. Steadman V. Sanford, the stadium construction broke ground in 1928. It cost $360,000 to build and was named after Dr. Sanford. The stadium opened on October 12, 1929, in a game against Yale University.

Sanford Stadium is famous for the **hedges** that surround it. Football games are said to be played "between the hedges." The hedges were included in the original design of the stadium and were planted in 1929.

The stadium has gone through six expansions over the years. The improvements have included building an upper deck and adding luxury suites. There was also an addition of a 36-by-73-foot (11-by-22-meter) scoreboard. In 2017, a $63-million **renovation** was approved. This included a new plaza and upgrades to the west side of the stadium. The renovation was completed before Georgia's first home game in 2018.

The hedges that surround the field at Sanford Stadium were completely removed in 2017 during renovations. Each one was carefully labeled, stored in a secret location, and then put back in its exact spot after the renovation was completed.

Where They Play

Welcome to Sanford Stadium, home of the Georgia Bulldogs. Overlooking the University of Georgia, it is considered one of the most beautiful stadiums in the National Collegiate Athletic Association (NCAA). Fans love to put on their red and white and cheer on the Dawgs as they dominate "between the hedges" each fall.

SEC WEST

1. **Auburn University**
   Auburn, Alabama
2. **Louisiana State University**
   Baton Rouge, Louisiana
3. **Mississippi State University**
   Starkville, Mississippi
4. **Texas A&M University**
   College Station, Texas
5. **University of Alabama**
   Tuscaloosa, Alabama
6. **University of Arkansas**
   Fayetteville, Arkansas
7. **University of Mississippi**
   Oxford, Mississippi

Arena
Sanford Stadium

Location
Athens, Georgia

Broke Ground
1928

Completed
1929

Surface
Real Grass

Features
- Tenth-largest stadium in the NCAA
- Seating capacity of 92,746
- Hosted soccer matches for the 1996 Olympic Games

SEC EAST

1. **University of Florida**
   Gainesville, Florida
2. ★ **University of Georgia**
   Athens, Georgia
3. **University of Kentucky**
   Lexington, Kentucky
4. **University of Missouri**
   Columbia, Missouri
5. **University of South Carolina**
   Columbia, South Carolina
6. **University of Tennessee**
   Knoxville, Tennessee
7. **Vanderbilt University**
   Nashville, Tennessee

NORTH DAKOTA
SOUTH DAKOTA
MINNESOTA
WISCONSIN
MICHIGAN
NEW YORK
PENNSYLVANIA
NEW HAMPSHIRE
VERMONT
MAINE
MASSACHUSETTS
RHODE ISLAND
CONNECTICUT
NEW JERSEY
DELAWARE
MARYLAND
WASHINGTON, D.C.
IOWA
NEBRASKA
ILLINOIS
INDIANA
OHIO
WEST VIRGINIA
VIRGINIA
KANSAS
MISSOURI
KENTUCKY
NORTH CAROLINA
TENNESSEE
SOUTH CAROLINA
OKLAHOMA
ARKANSAS
MISSISSIPPI
ALABAMA
GEORGIA
TEXAS
LOUISIANA
FLORIDA
Atlantic Ocean
Gulf of Mexico
1
2
3
4
5
6
7
SCALE
0 miles
500 miles
0 kilometers
500 km
LEGEND
Home Stadium
SEC West
SEC East
United States
Other Countries
Water

The Uniforms

Bulldogs players often wear **decals** on their helmets to bring **awareness** to different causes, or to remember a teammate who passed away.

The Bulldogs have a uniform contract with Nike through 2024. Nike creates uniforms for every athletic department at the University of Georgia.

During more than 100 years of Bulldogs football, the uniforms have gone through many changes. However, the key features have remained mostly the same since the 1980s. The uniforms consist of red jerseys, silver pants, and red helmets with a black "G."

Coach Butts introduced the pants that came to be known as "silver britches." Coach Dooley switched to white pants when he arrived, but reinstated the silver britches in 1980. The Bulldogs have worn silver pants ever since. Dooley also introduced the red helmets and is credited with the look of the uniform as it stands today.

Throughout the years, coaches have awarded helmet stickers to players for different accomplishments. White bones meant excellent on-field performance. Black bones stood for excellent academic performance. Players were also awarded black stars for being "Top Dog" of the game. Every coach has his own set of stickers, each with a different meaning.

The black and white bones on Bulldogs players' helmets are not permanent. They can be removed for poor performance on the field or bad grades on important assignments.

Student Athletes

Only **2 percent** of U.S. high school students are awarded **athletic scholarships.**

There are 110 players on Georgia's roster, but only about 70 travel with the team to SEC away games.

Being a college student athlete is hard work. Student athletes have to perform well on the football field and in the classroom. Georgia student athletes are required to meet a minimum grade point average and attend all of their classes. They must also have 12 academic credits per term. Georgia student athletes have access to academic mentoring and a tutorial program. UGA also offers many other services to help student athletes balance their lives.

Many student athletes are given athletic scholarships. An athletic scholarship is a financial aid agreement between the athlete and the college or university. Athletes who do not receive an athletic scholarship can be "walk-on" members of the team. This means they are on the team, but without athletic financial aid. UGA typically awards the maximum number of football scholarships allowed, which is 85.

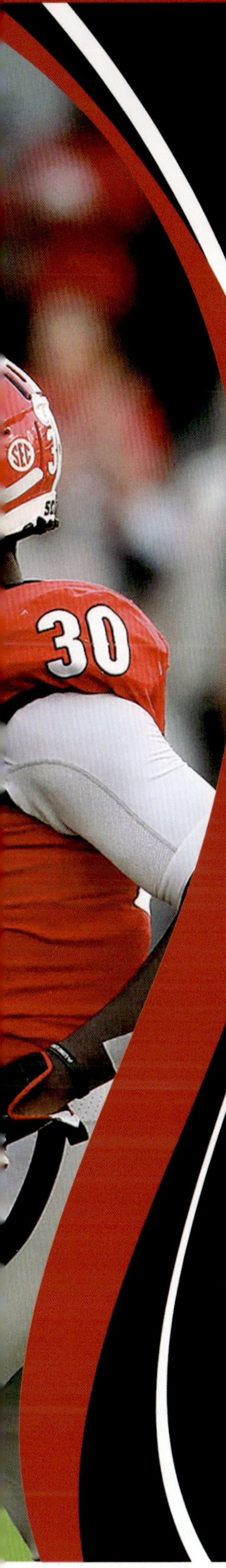

UGA quarterback Justin Fields was one of 2018's most highly recruited players. He originally committed to Pennsylvania State University but decommitted in order to play at Georgia, where he is also on the baseball team.

Bowl Games

There are **six** bowl games played on or around New Year's Day every year. They are called the **New Year's Six**.

Georgia's most recent Rose Bowl win was in 2018. The Bulldogs defeated the University of Oklahoma Sooners 54–48.

Bowl games are **postseason** games that count toward the national title claim. There are 40 college football bowl games in addition to the National Championship game. The bowl games happen after the conference championships. Since 2014, the College Football Playoff Selection Committee matches up four teams. These four teams compete in two semifinal bowl games. The winners of those games advance to the National Championship.

Georgia has played in 17 different bowls over the years, including the Sugar Bowl, the Orange Bowl, and the Capital One Bowl. The team has played in more than 50 bowl games and is tied for second for most bowl games ever played. UGA most recently won the Rose Bowl. The Bulldogs' bowl record is 31–21–3.

The Bulldogs have four Sugar Bowl trophies. Georgia's biggest Sugar Bowl victory was 41–10, over the University of Hawai'i Rainbow Warriors in 2008.

The Coaches

The Bulldogs have had **26 head coaches** since their first game in 1892.

Current UGA head coach Kirby Smart was a defensive back for the Bulldogs from 1995 to 1998.

Georgia football has been molded by a handful of long-term coaches. Wally Butts took over in 1939 and led the team to a 140–86–9 record. Vince Dooley took the reins in 1964, bringing the Bulldogs national recognition with his quarter century as a coach. Mark Richt had one of the best winning percentages in Georgia during his 15 seasons with the team.

WALLY BUTTS Coach Wally Butts coached the Bulldogs from 1939 to 1960. He led the Bulldogs to four SEC championships in 1942, 1946, 1948, and 1959. He coached notable players such as Frank Sinkwich and Charley Trippi, and coached the team to the 1942 National Championship. During that championship game, Georgia **shut out** the University of California, Los Angeles 9–0 in the Rose Bowl. Butts was inducted into the College Football Hall of Fame in 1997.

VINCE DOOLEY Vince Dooley is the best-known UGA coach, both because of how long he coached and because of his many victories. Under Coach Dooley, the Bulldogs won six SEC championships, many bowl games, and the 1980 National Championship. During his years as head coach from 1964 to 1988, Dooley's record was an impressive 201–77–10. He was named NCAA Coach of the Year in both 1980 and 1982.

MARK RICHT Mark Richt was head coach from 2001 to 2015. During this time, Georgia won two SEC championships, nine bowl games, and six SEC East finals. He was named SEC Coach of the Year in both 2002 and 2005. Richt was known for sending many players into the National Football League (NFL), and was the second-most winningest coach in program history.

The Mascot

Before Hairy Dawg made his first appearance at Sanford Stadium, he traveled with the Bulldogs to the Sugar Bowl, where they defeated the University of Notre Dame Fighting Irish in the National Championship game.

The Bulldogs have two dog mascots. Uga is a real dog, while Hairy Dawg is a person wearing a dog costume. Uga is an English bulldog. His name is the abbreviation of the University's name. There have been 10 Ugas. The first one debuted in 1956. Uga X is the current mascot. He wears a spiked collar and has a doghouse on the field. The previous nine Ugas are buried on the Sanford Stadium grounds.

Hairy Dawg debuted in 1981. He was created by mascot designer Tom Sapp. He was made to look rough and tough, with a large body and huge muscles. Hairy Dawg wears a red and black Bulldogs uniform and has a mean look on his face to scare the other team.

All 10 Ugas have come from the Seiler family in Savannah, Georgia. Sonny Seiler is a UGA alumni, and the first Uga was his pet.

Legends of the Past

For many players, their time with the Bulldogs is the start of a promising football career. These are some of the best-known football players to play for the University of Georgia.

Herschel Walker

Herschel Walker was one of the all-time great Bulldogs football players. As a college junior, he led Georgia to an 11–0 regular season, and he went on to win the Heisman Trophy. Walker went pro after his junior season, landing a spot on the New Jersey Generals of the U.S. Football League. He was **drafted** by the Dallas Cowboys in 1985. During his time in the NFL, Walker had 8,225 rushing yards and 4,859 receiving yards. He retired in 1997.

Position: Running Back
Seasons: 1980–1982 (Georgia Bulldogs), 1983–1985 (New Jersey Generals), 1986–1989 (Dallas Cowboys), 1989–1991 (Minnesota Vikings), 1992–1994 (Philadelphia Eagles), 1995 (New York Giants), 1996–1997 (Dallas Cowboys)
Born: March 3, 1962, Wrightsville, Georgia

Frank Sinkwich

Frank Sinkwich was one of Georgia's leading halfbacks. During his time at Georgia, he was a two-time All-American and won the Heisman Trophy. He helped the Bulldogs win both an Orange Bowl and a Rose Bowl. Sinkwich was a first-round draft pick by the Detroit Lions. During his time with the Lions, he was named an **All-Pro** twice and the league **Most Valuable Player (MVP)** in 1944. Sinkwich later played with the New York Yankees of the All-America Football Conference. He was eventually traded to the Baltimore Colts. He retired in 1947 and was inducted into the College Football Hall of Fame in 1954.

Position: Halfback
Seasons: 1940–1942 (Georgia Bulldogs), 1943–1944 (Detroit Lions), 1946–1947 (New York Yankees), 1947 (Baltimore Colts)
Born: October 10, 1920, Zagreb, Croatia

Champ Bailey

Champ Bailey was a speedy cornerback from Georgia. In his sophomore year at UGA, he helped the Bulldogs earn their way to a 9–2 season. After his impressive junior year, he was voted first-team All-SEC and an All-American. Bailey was a number seven draft pick by the Washington Redskins in 1999. He went on to have a successful career in the NFL with a total of 812 tackles and 52 interceptions. He was selected to play in the **Pro Bowl** 12 times. In 2004, Bailey was traded to the Denver Broncos, where he played until his retirement in 2013.

Position: Cornerback
Seasons: 1996–1998 (Georgia Bulldogs), 1999–2003 (Washington Redskins), 2004–2013 (Denver Broncos)
Born: June 22, 1978, Folkston, Georgia

Todd Gurley

Todd Gurley played football at UGA under Coach Richt. During his time there, he was named both first team and second team All-SEC. He skipped his college senior year to play in the NFL. Gurley was drafted as a 10th pick overall by the St. Louis Rams in the 2015 draft. During his time with the Rams, he has had 955 carries, 40 rushing touchdowns, and 4,096 rushing yards. In 2018, Gurley signed a five-year contract extension with the Rams.

Position: Running Back
Seasons: 2012–2014 (Georgia Bulldogs), 2015–2016 (St. Louis Rams), 2016–Present (Los Angeles Rams)
Born: August 3, 1994, Baltimore, Maryland

All-Time Records

36
Career Sacks
David Pollack's 36 career **sacks** are a UGA record, and the third highest in NCAA history.

170
Tackles in a Season
Knox Culpepper's UGA single-season tackle record of 170 in 1984 still stands today.

137
Career Touchdowns
Between 2010 and 2013, Aaron Murray set several UGA and SEC records, including the Bulldogs' career touchdowns record of 137.

467

Career Tackles

Ben Zambiasi set the current UGA record for career tackles, with 467 from 1975 to 1977.

5,259

Rushing Yards in a Season

Herschel Walker is the only player in SEC history to run for more than 5,000 yards, with a career record of 5,259.

Timeline

Throughout the team's history, the Georgia Bulldogs have had many memorable events that have become defining moments for the team and its fans.

1942
Frank Sinkwich becomes Georgia's first Heisman Trophy winner.

On January 30, 1892, the Bulldogs play their first game against Mercer University.

1880 | 1900 | 1920 | 1940

1892
Georgia plays Auburn, the first game of what is now thought of as the South's oldest college football rivalry.

1893
The very first game of the in-state rivalry between Georgia and Georgia Tech, known as "Clean, Old-Fashioned Hate," is played.

1929
The famous hedges that surround the UGA field are planted.

1943
The Bulldogs win their first National Championship game.

1981
Georgia wins its second National Championship game.

1982
Herschel Walker wins the Heisman Trophy.

The Future

Exciting things are happening for the Georgia Bulldogs. In 2016, their record was 8–5, and they were tied for second in the SEC. The 2017 season brought them both the SEC East and the SEC championship titles. Heading into the 2018 season, Coach Smart was hitting his stride and many polls named Georgia as a top-ranked team.

1960 1980 2000 2020

On November 8, 1980, Lindsay Scott catches a throw and runs 92 yards to win the game. The famous play is known as "Run, Lindsay, Run."

1963
Vince Dooley is hired as the new head coach.

2018
The University of Georgia Bulldogs defeat the University of Oklahoma Sooners in the Rose Bowl.

Write a Biography

Life Story

A person's life story can be the subject of a book. This kind of book is called a biography. Biographies often describe the lives of people who have achieved great success. These people may be alive today, or they may have lived many years ago. Reading a biography can help you learn more about a great person.

Get the Facts

Use this book, and research in the library and on the internet, to find out more about your favorite player. Learn as much about him as you can. What position does he play? What are his statistics in important categories? Has he set any records? Also, be sure to write down key events in the person's life. What was his childhood like? What has he accomplished off the field? Is there anything else that makes this person special or unusual?

Use the Concept Web

A concept web is a useful research tool. Read the questions in the concept web on the following page. Answer the questions in your notebook. Your answers will help you write a biography.

Concept Web

Write a Biography

Adulthood
- Where does this individual currently reside?
- Does he have a family?

Your Opinion
- What did you learn from the books you read in your research?
- Would you suggest these books to others?
- Was anything missing from these books?

Childhood
- Where and when was he born?
- Describe his parents, siblings, and friends.
- Did he grow up in unusual circumstances?

Accomplishments off the Field
- What is this person's life's work?
- Has he received awards or recognition for accomplishments?
- How have this person's accomplishments served others?

Help and Obstacles
- Did this individual have a positive attitude?
- Did he receive help from others?
- Did this person have a mentor?
- Did this person face any hardships?
- If so, how were the hardships overcome?

Accomplishments on the Field
- What records does this person hold?
- What key games and plays have defined his career?
- What are his stats in categories important to his position?

Work and Preparation
- What was this person's education?
- What was his work experience?
- How does this person work?
- What is the process he uses?

Trivia Time

Take this quiz to test your knowledge of the Georgia Bulldogs. The answers are printed upside down under each question.

1 What does the term "between the hedges" mean?

A. It refers to football games played at the University of Georgia

2 What type of animal is Uga, the team mascot?

A. An English bulldog

3 What is the name of the Bulldogs' stadium?

A. Sanford Stadium

4 What is the term for the UGA–Georgia Tech rivalry?

A. Clean, Old-Fashioned Hate

5 Which letter is printed on the Bulldogs' helmets?

A. A "G"

6 Who coached Georgia for 25 years?

A. Vince Dooley

7 What is known as "the South's oldest college football rivalry?"

A. UGA vs. Auburn

8 Where are the first nine Ugas buried?

A. On the Sanford Stadium grounds

9 What is the name of the famous play made by Lindsay Scott?

A. "Run, Lindsay, Run"

10 Who was the very first UGA head coach?

A. Dr. Charles Herty

Key Words

All-Pro: a term used to designate the best players of each position during a given season

drafted: chosen to play professionally in the National Football League during an annual event

hedges: fences made of bushes grown close together

Heisman Memorial Trophy: an annual award given to the college football player who best demonstrates excellence and hard work

Most Valuable Player (MVP): the player judged to be most valuable to his team's success

postseason: a sporting event that takes place after the end of the regular season

Pro Bowl: the annual all-star game for NFL players pitting the best players in the National Football Conference against the best players in the American Football Conference

renovation: construction that works to improve or expand an older building

rivalries: competitions between different groups or individuals toward the same objective or goal

sacks: when the quarterback, or another offensive player acting as a passer, is tackled behind the line of scrimmage before he can throw a forward pass

shut out: to not allow an opposing team to score any points

Index

Log on to www.av2books.com

AV² by Weigl brings you media enhanced books that support active learning. Go to www.av2books.com, and enter the special code found on page 2 of this book. You will gain access to enriched and enhanced content that supplements and complements this book. Content includes video, audio, weblinks, quizzes, a slideshow, and activities.

AV² Online Navigation

Audio
Listen to sections o
the book read alou

Book Pages
AV² pages directly correspond to pages in the book.

Video
Watch informative video clips.

Embedded Weblinks
Gain additional information for research.

Key Words
Study vocabulary, and complete a matching word activity.

Try This!
Complete activities and hands-on experiments.

Quizzes
Test your knowledge.

Slideshow
View images and captions, and prepare a presentation.